Carl Cuesta

Not Boring
Ultimate Guide to
SBA 7a and 504 Financing
in Healthcare

Table Of Contents

Chapter 1: Introduction to SBA 7a and 504 Financing in Healthcare

5

The Importance of Financing in the Healthcare Industry

5

Overview of SBA 7a and 504 Loans

7

Benefits of SBA 7a and 504 Financing for Small Businesses in Healthcare

8

Chapter 2: Eligibility and Qualifications for SBA 7a and 504 Loans

10

General Eligibility Requirements for Small Businesses

10

Specific Qualifications for Healthcare Industry Businesses

12

Understanding Credit Scores and Requirements

14

Financial Documentations and Requirements

16

Chapter 3: SBA 7a Loan Program for Healthcare Businesses

19

Key Features and Benefits of SBA 7a Loans

19

Loan Amounts, Interest Rates, and Terms

21

Eligible Expenses for SBA 7a Financing in Healthcare

22

Application Process for SBA 7a Loans in Healthcare

25

Chapter 4: SBA 504 Loan Program for Healthcare Businesses

27

Key Features and Benefits of SBA 504 Loans

27

Loan Amounts, Interest Rates, and Terms

29

Eligible Expenses for SBA 504 Financing in Healthcare

31

Application Process for SBA 504 Loans in Healthcare

33

Chapter 5: Choosing the Right Loan Program for Your Healthcare Business

34

Evaluating Your Healthcare Business's Financial Needs

34

Assessing Your Business's Qualifications for SBA 7a vs. 504 Loans

36

Understanding the Impact of Loan Terms on Your Healthcare Business

38

Comparing Interest Rates and Fees for SBA 7a and 504 Loans

41

Chapter 6: Tips for a Successful Loan Application in Healthcare

42

Preparing Financial Documents and Projections

42

Building Solid Credit History and Score

44

Selecting the Right Lender for Your Healthcare Business

47

Navigating the Application Process and Timelines

49

Chapter 7: Managing SBA 7a and 504 Loan Repayments in Healthcare

51

Understanding Loan Repayment Terms and Conditions

51

Budgeting and Cash Flow Management for Healthcare Businesses

53

Strategies for Loan Repayment and Debt Management

55

Dealing with Loan Default and Other Challenges

57

Chapter 8: Case Studies: Successful Healthcare Businesses with SBA Financing

59

Case Study 1: Dr. Smith's Primary Care Clinic

59

Case Study 2: OptiCare Vision Center

61

Case Study 3: Dental Solutions Group

63

Case Study 4: Accounting Solutions for Healthcare Providers

65

Chapter 9: Additional Resources and Support for Healthcare Businesses

67

Government Programs and Initiatives for Healthcare Businesses

67

Partnering with Industry Associations and Organizations

70

Professional Services and Consultants for Healthcare Businesses

72

Continuing Education and Training Opportunities in Healthcare Financing

74

Chapter 10: Conclusion

76

Recap of Key Points and Takeaways

76

Final Thoughts on SBA 7a and 504 Financing in Healthcare

78

Empowering Small Business Owners in the Healthcare Industry

80

Chapter 1: Introduction to SBA 7a and 504 Financing in Healthcare

The Importance of Financing in the Healthcare Industry

The Importance of Financing in the Healthcare Industry

In the fast-paced and ever-evolving world of healthcare, financing plays a crucial role in ensuring the success and growth of small businesses. Whether you're a primary care doctor, optometrist, dentist, or accountant in the healthcare industry, understanding the importance of financing is vital to achieving your business goals. This subchapter will delve into the significance of SBA 7a and 504 financing for small businesses in the healthcare industry, providing valuable insights and guidance.

One of the key reasons financing is essential is the high cost associated with starting and expanding healthcare businesses. From acquiring state-of-the-art medical equipment to renovating and expanding facilities, the financial burden can be overwhelming. SBA 7a and 504 financing options specifically cater to small businesses in the healthcare industry, offering accessible and affordable funding solutions. These financing programs can provide the capital needed to invest in technology, hire skilled staff, and expand services, ultimately improving patient care and satisfaction.

Moreover, financing allows small businesses to stay competitive in the ever-evolving healthcare landscape. With advancements in medical technology and treatments, it is crucial for healthcare providers to stay up-to-date to deliver the best care. However, these innovations often come with a hefty price tag. Through SBA 7a and 504 financing, small businesses can access the funds required to invest in cutting-edge equipment, software, and training, enabling them to provide superior services and attract more patients.

Additionally, financing empowers small businesses to seize growth opportunities and overcome challenges. Whether it's expanding to a new location, hiring additional staff, or implementing new services, having access to capital is essential. The healthcare industry is highly competitive, and small businesses need to adapt and innovate to thrive. SBA 7a and 504 financing can provide the necessary funds to take advantage of opportunities and navigate through difficult times, ensuring long-term sustainability.

Furthermore, financing offers tax benefits and favorable terms, making it an attractive option for small businesses in the healthcare industry. SBA 7a and 504 loans often have lower interest rates, longer repayment terms, and reduced down payment requirements, relieving the financial strain on healthcare providers. Additionally, the interest on these loans may be tax-deductible, further reducing the overall cost of financing.

In conclusion, financing is of paramount importance in the healthcare industry for small business owners, primary care doctors, optometrists, dentists, and accountants. SBA 7a and 504 financing provide the necessary capital to start, expand, and remain competitive in this dynamic sector. By embracing financing options, healthcare businesses can invest in technology, attract more patients, seize growth opportunities, and ultimately deliver exceptional care to their communities.

Overview of SBA 7a and 504 Loans

Overview of SBA 7a and 504 Loans

As a small business owner in the healthcare industry, you may often find yourself in need of financial assistance to grow your practice or invest in new equipment and technology. Thankfully, the Small Business Administration (SBA) offers two primary loan programs specifically designed to support small businesses like yours – the SBA 7a and 504 loans.

The SBA 7a loan program is one of the most popular financing options for small businesses. It provides flexible terms and affordable interest rates, making it an attractive choice for healthcare professionals looking to expand their operations. With an SBA 7a loan, you can use the funds for a variety of purposes, such as purchasing real estate, renovating existing facilities, acquiring new equipment, or even refinancing existing debt. The loan amount can go up to $5 million, giving you the financial flexibility necessary to meet your business goals.

On the other hand, the SBA 504 loan program primarily focuses on assisting small businesses in acquiring real estate and large equipment. It offers long-term fixed-rate financing with low down payments, making it an excellent option for healthcare providers looking to purchase or renovate their own buildings or invest in expensive medical equipment. The SBA 504 loan program is unique in that it involves a partnership between a Certified Development Company (CDC), a traditional lender, and the SBA. This partnership ensures that you receive favorable loan terms and reduced risk.

Both the SBA 7a and 504 loans offer competitive interest rates and longer repayment terms compared to conventional loans. Additionally, they provide small business owners with the opportunity to gain access to capital that may otherwise be difficult to obtain from traditional lenders. These SBA loan programs have been instrumental in helping healthcare professionals, including primary care doctors, optometrists, dentists, and accountants, to start, expand, and modernize their practices.

Understanding the nuances of SBA 7a and 504 loans is crucial for small business owners in the healthcare industry. In this book, "The Ultimate Guide to SBA 7a and 504 Financing in Healthcare," we will delve deeper into the specifics of these loan programs. We will explore the eligibility requirements, application process, and the key factors that lenders consider when evaluating loan applications. By the end of this guide, you will have a comprehensive understanding of how SBA 7a and 504 loans can help you achieve your business goals in the healthcare industry.

Benefits of SBA 7a and 504 Financing for Small Businesses in Healthcare

Benefits of SBA 7a and 504 Financing for Small Businesses in Healthcare

Small business owners in the healthcare industry face unique challenges when it comes to securing financing for their ventures. However, with the introduction of Small Business Administration (SBA) loan programs like the 7a and 504 financing, these entrepreneurs now have access to valuable resources that can help them grow and succeed.

One of the major benefits of SBA 7a and 504 financing for small businesses in healthcare is the availability of long-term, low-interest loans. These loans provide small business owners with the necessary capital to start or expand their healthcare practices. The low-interest rates make it easier for these entrepreneurs to manage their finances and repay the loan over an extended period of time.

Additionally, SBA loans offer flexible terms and repayment options. Small business owners in the healthcare industry can choose from a variety of loan structures that best suit their needs. Whether it's financing for equipment, real estate, or working capital, the SBA 7a and 504 programs can be tailored to meet the specific requirements of healthcare professionals.

Another advantage of SBA 7a and 504 financing is the lower down payment requirement. Traditional lenders often demand a substantial down payment, making it difficult for small business owners to secure the necessary funds. However, the SBA programs require a significantly lower down payment, reducing the financial burden on healthcare entrepreneurs.

Furthermore, SBA loans come with certain benefits that are exclusive to these programs. For example, borrowers can enjoy longer repayment terms, which can alleviate the pressure of monthly payments and allow for better cash flow management. Additionally, SBA loans do not require collateral for amounts up to $25,000, providing small business owners with peace of mind.

Small business owners in the healthcare industry can also benefit from the expertise and guidance provided by SBA-approved lenders. These lenders have a deep understanding of the healthcare sector and can offer valuable insights and assistance throughout the loan application process. From helping entrepreneurs prepare the necessary documentation to advising on the best loan options available, SBA-approved lenders can be invaluable resources.

In conclusion, SBA 7a and 504 financing offers numerous benefits for small business owners in the healthcare industry. From low-interest rates and flexible repayment terms to reduced down payment requirements and expert guidance, these loan programs provide the necessary support for entrepreneurs to thrive in the healthcare sector. Whether you're a primary care doctor, optometrist, dentist, or accountant looking to start or expand your healthcare practice, exploring SBA loan options can be a game-changer in your journey to success.

Chapter 2: Eligibility and Qualifications for SBA 7a and 504 Loans

General Eligibility Requirements for Small Businesses

General Eligibility Requirements for Small Businesses

When it comes to accessing SBA 7a and 504 financing for small businesses in the healthcare industry, there are certain eligibility requirements that small business owners, primary care doctors, optometrists, dentists, and accountants need to meet. Understanding these requirements is essential for successfully obtaining the financing needed to grow and expand your healthcare business.

First and foremost, the Small Business Administration (SBA) defines small businesses based on the industry in which they operate. In the healthcare industry, the size standards can vary depending on the specific type of business. For example, a primary care doctor's office may have different size standards compared to a dental clinic or an optometry practice. It is important to review the SBA's size standards for your specific healthcare niche to ensure that your business qualifies as a small business.

Additionally, small businesses seeking SBA 7a and 504 financing must be for-profit entities located in the United States. Non-profit organizations, foreign-owned businesses, and businesses engaged in lending or investment activities are generally not eligible for SBA financing.

Furthermore, small businesses must demonstrate the ability to repay the loan. This typically involves providing financial statements, tax returns, and other documentation to prove the business's cash flow and profitability. Lenders will closely evaluate the business's financial health and creditworthiness to determine if it meets the repayment requirements.

Another important requirement is that the small business must be able to demonstrate that it has exhausted all other financing options before seeking SBA financing. This means that the business owner must show that they have approached traditional lenders, such as banks, and have been unable to secure the necessary funding.

Finally, it is crucial for small businesses to have a solid business plan in place. A comprehensive business plan outlines the company's objectives, strategies, market analysis, and financial projections. This document demonstrates to lenders that the business has a clear vision and a viable plan for success.

In conclusion, small businesses in the healthcare industry seeking SBA 7a and 504 financing must meet specific eligibility requirements. These requirements include being classified as a small business within the healthcare industry, being a for-profit entity located in the United States, demonstrating the ability to repay the loan, exhausting other financing options, and having a well-developed business plan. By understanding and meeting these eligibility requirements, small business owners, primary care doctors, optometrists, dentists, and accountants can increase their chances of obtaining the necessary financing to grow and thrive in the healthcare industry.

Specific Qualifications for Healthcare Industry Businesses

Specific Qualifications for Healthcare Industry Businesses

When it comes to securing SBA 7a and 504 financing for small businesses in the healthcare industry, there are several specific qualifications that businesses need to meet. Understanding these requirements is vital for small business owners, primary care doctors, optometrists, dentists, and accountants who are looking to expand or establish their healthcare practices.

One of the primary qualifications for healthcare industry businesses seeking SBA financing is the need for a solid business plan. This plan should outline the unique aspects of your healthcare business, including its target market, competition analysis, growth projections, and marketing strategies. Having a well-thought-out business plan demonstrates to lenders that you have a clear vision for your practice and are capable of managing finances responsibly.

Another crucial qualification is a strong credit history. Lenders will review your personal and business credit scores to assess your creditworthiness. While a perfect credit score is not always necessary, having a good credit history and a solid repayment track record will greatly increase your chances of securing financing. It is essential to review your credit reports and address any discrepancies or negative marks before applying for a loan.

Furthermore, lenders will evaluate your industry experience and expertise. Demonstrating your knowledge and experience in the healthcare industry is crucial, as it instills confidence in lenders that you understand the unique challenges and opportunities within the sector. Providing evidence of your education, certifications, and relevant work experience will strengthen your loan application.

Collateral is also an important factor in securing SBA financing for healthcare businesses. Lenders typically require collateral to secure the loan, which can include real estate, equipment, or other assets. Having valuable collateral can help mitigate the lender's risk and increase your chances of loan approval.

Lastly, lenders will assess your ability to generate sufficient cash flow to repay the loan. They will analyze your financial statements, including profit and loss statements, balance sheets, and cash flow projections. It is essential to demonstrate consistent and reliable cash flow to convince lenders that you can meet your financial obligations.

In conclusion, meeting the specific qualifications for healthcare industry businesses seeking SBA 7a and 504 financing is essential for small business owners, primary care doctors, optometrists, dentists, and accountants looking to secure funding. A well-crafted business plan, strong credit history, industry expertise, valuable collateral, and a proven ability to generate cash flow are all key factors that lenders consider when evaluating loan applications. By understanding and addressing these qualifications, healthcare businesses can enhance their chances of obtaining the necessary financing to grow and thrive in the competitive healthcare industry.

Understanding Credit Scores and Requirements

Understanding Credit Scores and Requirements

As a small business owner in the healthcare industry, it is crucial to have a good understanding of credit scores and requirements when seeking SBA 7a and 504 financing. Your credit score plays a significant role in determining your eligibility for loans and the terms you may be offered. This subchapter aims to provide you with a comprehensive overview of credit scores and the requirements you need to meet to secure financing for your healthcare business.

Credit scores are numerical representations of your creditworthiness and financial history. Lenders use these scores to assess the risk associated with lending you money. The most widely used credit score is the FICO score, which ranges from 300 to 850. A higher score indicates lower credit risk and increases your chances of securing favorable loan terms.

To qualify for SBA 7a and 504 financing, you generally need a credit score of 680 or higher. However, some lenders may accept lower scores depending on other factors such as your business's financial health and your personal assets. It's essential to review your credit report regularly to identify any discrepancies or errors that could negatively impact your score. Taking steps to improve your credit score, such as paying bills on time and reducing debt, can significantly enhance your chances of obtaining financing.

In addition to credit scores, lenders also consider your credit history, debt-to-income ratio, and collateral when evaluating loan applications. A solid credit history with a track record of responsible borrowing strengthens your application. Lenders also assess your debt-to-income ratio to ensure that you can comfortably repay the loan without straining your finances.

Collateral is another important factor when seeking SBA 7a and 504 financing. While these programs offer favorable terms and lower down payments, lenders still require collateral to secure the loan. Collateral can include real estate, equipment, or other assets that can be liquidated if you default on the loan.

Understanding credit scores and requirements is crucial for small business owners in the healthcare industry seeking SBA 7a and 504 financing. Maintaining a good credit score, having a solid credit history, managing your debt-to-income ratio, and offering suitable collateral are key to securing favorable loan terms. Regularly reviewing your credit report and taking steps to improve your creditworthiness will increase your chances of obtaining the financing needed to grow and expand your healthcare business.

Financial Documentations and Requirements

Financial Documentations and Requirements

When it comes to securing financing for your small healthcare business, it is crucial to understand the financial documentations and requirements that lenders typically expect. This subchapter will provide you with a comprehensive guide on the necessary financial documentation and requirements for SBA 7a and 504 financing in the healthcare industry.

1. Personal and Business Financial Statements:
Lenders will require both personal and business financial statements to evaluate your creditworthiness. These statements provide a clear picture of your personal and business financial health, including assets, liabilities, income, and expenses.

2. Business Plan:

A well-crafted business plan is essential to secure financing. It outlines your business goals, target market, marketing strategies, and financial projections. Lenders want to see a solid plan that demonstrates your understanding of the healthcare industry and your ability to generate revenue.

3. Tax Returns:

Lenders will review your personal and business tax returns for the past two to three years. This helps them assess your historical financial performance, identify any potential red flags, and determine your ability to repay the loan.

4. Debt Schedule:

A comprehensive debt schedule provides lenders with a detailed overview of your existing debts, including loans, leases, and lines of credit. This document helps them assess your debt-to-income ratio and your ability to handle additional debt.

5. Collateral Documentation:

Depending on the financing program, lenders may require collateral to secure the loan. Collateral can include real estate, equipment, or other business assets. Documentation such as property appraisals, equipment valuations, and insurance policies will be required to evaluate the collateral's value.

6. Financial Projections:

Lenders want to see your future financial projections to assess your ability to generate sufficient cash flow and repay the loan. Projections should include income statements, balance sheets, and cash flow statements for at least three years.

7. Industry-specific Documentation:

As a healthcare business, you may be required to provide specific documentation related to your industry. This can include licenses, certifications, contracts with insurance providers, and any other relevant documents that demonstrate your compliance and legitimacy.

By understanding and preparing these financial documentations and requirements, you will position yourself as a credible and reliable candidate for SBA 7a and 504 financing. Take the time to gather and organize these documents before approaching lenders, as it will streamline the application process and increase your chances of securing the funding you need to grow and succeed in the healthcare industry.

Chapter 3: SBA 7a Loan Program for Healthcare Businesses

Key Features and Benefits of SBA 7a Loans

Key Features and Benefits of SBA 7a Loans

When it comes to financing options for small businesses in the healthcare industry, the Small Business Administration (SBA) 7a loan program offers a range of key features and benefits. As a small business owner in the healthcare industry, whether you are a primary care doctor, optometrist, dentist, or accountant, understanding these features can help you make informed decisions about your financing needs.

1. Flexible Loan Amounts: SBA 7a loans provide small businesses in the healthcare industry with access to a wide range of loan amounts, making it suitable for businesses of varying sizes. Whether you need a small loan to cover working capital or a larger loan to fund expansion plans, the SBA 7a program can offer the financing you need.

2. Longer Repayment Terms: Unlike traditional bank loans, SBA 7a loans typically come with longer repayment terms, often ranging from 10 to 25 years. This allows small businesses in the healthcare industry to have more manageable monthly payments and better cash flow management.

3. Lower Down Payments: One of the most attractive features of SBA 7a loans is the lower down payment requirement. Typically, the down payment for an SBA 7a loan is around 10%, which is significantly lower than the 20% or more required by conventional lenders. This feature allows small business owners in the healthcare industry to preserve their working capital while still accessing the necessary funds.

4. Competitive Interest Rates: SBA 7a loans offer competitive interest rates, which can be fixed or variable. The SBA sets a maximum interest rate that lenders can charge, ensuring that small business owners in the healthcare industry have access to affordable financing options.

5. Multiple Use of Funds: SBA 7a loans provide small businesses in the healthcare industry with the flexibility to use the funds for various purposes. Whether you need to purchase new equipment, expand your practice, hire new staff, or refinance existing debt, an SBA 7a loan can accommodate your needs.

6. SBA Guarantee: One of the major benefits of the SBA 7a loan program is the SBA guarantee. This guarantee reduces the risk for lenders, making it easier for small businesses in the healthcare industry to qualify for financing, even if they have limited collateral or less established credit histories.

In summary, the SBA 7a loan program offers small business owners in the healthcare industry a range of key features and benefits. From flexible loan amounts and longer repayment terms to lower down payments and competitive interest rates, these loans provide the necessary funding for growth and expansion. Whether you are a primary care doctor, optometrist, dentist, or accountant, understanding the features and benefits of SBA 7a loans can help you navigate the financing landscape and make informed decisions for your healthcare business.

Loan Amounts, Interest Rates, and Terms

Loan Amounts, Interest Rates, and Terms

One of the most important aspects of obtaining financing for small businesses in the healthcare industry is understanding the loan amounts, interest rates, and terms associated with SBA 7a and 504 financing. Whether you are a small business owner, primary care doctor, optometrist, dentist, or accountant, this subchapter will provide you with valuable insights into securing the right loan for your healthcare business.

Loan amounts vary depending on the type of loan you choose. SBA 7a loans generally have a maximum loan amount of $5 million, whereas SBA 504 loans can go as high as $20 million. The loan amount you qualify for is often determined by factors such as your creditworthiness, business plan, and collateral. It is essential to carefully assess your financial needs and work with a knowledgeable lender to determine the appropriate loan amount for your healthcare business.

Interest rates are a crucial factor to consider when seeking financing. SBA 7a loans typically have variable interest rates tied to the prime rate, plus a margin. These rates are often competitive compared to traditional bank loans, making them an attractive option for healthcare businesses. On the other hand, SBA 504 loans have fixed interest rates, providing stability and predictability over the loan term. Working with an experienced lender who specializes in healthcare financing can help you secure favorable interest rates that suit your financial goals.

Understanding the loan terms is vital to ensure a successful financing experience. SBA 7a loans typically have longer terms, ranging from 7 to 25 years, allowing for more manageable monthly payments. Alternatively, SBA 504 loans have terms that vary depending on the use of funds. For real estate acquisitions, the term can be as long as 25 years, while for equipment purchases, the term can go up to 10 years. It is essential to carefully evaluate your healthcare business's cash flow projections and choose a loan term that aligns with your financial capabilities.

In conclusion, when seeking financing for your healthcare business, it is crucial to understand the loan amounts, interest rates, and terms associated with SBA 7a and 504 financing. By working with a lender experienced in healthcare financing, you can navigate the complex world of loans and secure the funding needed to grow and thrive in the healthcare industry. Remember to assess your financial needs, evaluate interest rates, and choose loan terms that align with your business goals. With the right financing, you can take your healthcare business to new heights of success.

Eligible Expenses for SBA 7a Financing in Healthcare

Eligible Expenses for SBA 7a Financing in Healthcare

One of the biggest challenges faced by small business owners in the healthcare industry is securing funding for their practice or facility. Fortunately, the Small Business Administration (SBA) offers various financing options, including the SBA 7a loan program, specifically designed to support small businesses in the healthcare sector. Understanding the eligible expenses under this program is crucial for healthcare professionals looking to expand their practice, purchase new equipment, or refinance existing debt.

When applying for SBA 7a financing in healthcare, small business owners can utilize the funds for a wide range of expenses. These include:

1. Practice Acquisitions: Whether you are a primary care doctor, optometrist, or dentist looking to acquire an existing practice, the SBA 7a loan can be used to finance the purchase. This includes the cost of acquiring the practice, equipment, and even working capital needed for a smooth transition.

2. Equipment and Technology: Staying up-to-date with the latest medical equipment and technology is crucial for the success of any healthcare practice. SBA 7a financing can be used to purchase or upgrade medical equipment, software systems, electronic health records (EHRs), and other technological advancements necessary for providing quality patient care.

3. Leasehold Improvements: If you are planning to renovate or remodel your existing healthcare facility, SBA 7a financing can cover the costs of leasehold improvements. This includes upgrading the waiting area, treatment rooms, signage, and other structural modifications required to enhance the patient experience.

4. Debt Refinancing: Many healthcare professionals find themselves burdened with high-interest debts. The SBA 7a loan program allows small business owners to refinance existing debts, providing the opportunity to reduce monthly payments, extend the loan term, and potentially improve cash flow.

5. Working Capital: SBA 7a financing can also be used to cover day-to-day operational expenses, such as payroll, rent, utilities, inventory, and marketing. Having access to working capital ensures that healthcare practices can continue providing quality services while managing their financial obligations.

It is important to note that while the SBA 7a loan program offers flexibility in terms of eligible expenses, it is vital to consult with an experienced lender or financial advisor who specializes in SBA financing for healthcare businesses. They can guide you through the loan application process, help determine the loan amount you qualify for, and ensure that you are utilizing the funds in a way that maximizes the growth and success of your healthcare practice.

In conclusion, the SBA 7a loan program provides an excellent opportunity for small business owners in the healthcare industry to access the funding they need to grow and thrive. Understanding the eligible expenses is crucial for healthcare professionals looking to leverage this financing option and take their practice to the next level.

Application Process for SBA 7a Loans in Healthcare

Application Process for SBA 7a Loans in Healthcare

For small business owners in the healthcare industry, securing financing can be a daunting task. However, the Small Business Administration (SBA) offers a range of loan programs specifically tailored to meet the needs of healthcare businesses. One of the most popular options is the SBA 7a loan, which provides funding for working capital, equipment purchase, and even real estate acquisition. This subchapter will guide small business owners, primary care doctors, optometrists, dentists, and accountants through the application process for SBA 7a loans in the healthcare industry.

Before delving into the specifics of the application process, it is important to understand the benefits of SBA 7a loans. These loans offer longer repayment terms, lower down payments, and competitive interest rates, making them an attractive financing option for small businesses in the healthcare sector. Moreover, SBA loans are guaranteed by the government, which reduces the risk for lenders and increases the chances of approval.

The application process for SBA 7a loans typically involves several steps. First, potential borrowers must gather all the necessary documents, including financial statements, tax returns, business plans, and personal background information. These documents will be used to assess the creditworthiness of the business and its owners.

Next, small business owners should find a lender who is approved by the SBA to offer 7a loans. It is advisable to choose a lender with experience in the healthcare industry, as they will have a better understanding of the unique challenges and opportunities within the sector.

Once a lender has been selected, the application can be submitted along with the required documentation. The lender will then evaluate the application and conduct a thorough review of the business's financials, credit history, and repayment ability. This process may take some time, so it is important to be patient and responsive to any requests for additional information or clarifications.

If the application is approved, the borrower will receive a loan offer outlining the terms and conditions of the loan. It is crucial to carefully review this offer and seek professional advice if needed. Once the loan offer is accepted, the borrower will need to complete the necessary paperwork and fulfill any remaining requirements before receiving the funds.

In conclusion, the application process for SBA 7a loans in the healthcare industry can be complex, but with the right guidance and preparation, small business owners, primary care doctors, optometrists, dentists, and accountants can successfully secure the financing they need to grow and thrive. By understanding the requirements and diligently completing the necessary steps, healthcare businesses can take advantage of the benefits offered by SBA loans and propel their growth in the ever-evolving healthcare industry.

Chapter 4: SBA 504 Loan Program for Healthcare Businesses

Key Features and Benefits of SBA 504 Loans

Key Features and Benefits of SBA 504 Loans

For small business owners in the healthcare industry, obtaining financing can be a daunting task. Traditional loans often come with high interest rates and strict eligibility criteria, making it challenging to secure the necessary funds for growth and expansion. However, there is a solution that specifically caters to the needs of small businesses in healthcare – SBA 504 loans. In this subchapter, we will explore the key features and benefits of SBA 504 loans, outlining why they are an excellent financing option for primary care doctors, optometrists, dentists, and accountants in the healthcare industry.

One of the standout features of SBA 504 loans is the low down payment requirement. With as little as 10% down, small business owners can access the capital they need to invest in new equipment, expand their facilities, or even acquire real estate. This low down payment allows healthcare professionals to preserve their working capital and allocate it towards other critical business needs.

Additionally, SBA 504 loans offer long-term fixed interest rates. This stability provides small business owners with predictability and peace of mind when it comes to their monthly loan payments. With interest rates typically lower than those offered by traditional lenders, healthcare professionals can save significant amounts of money over the life of the loan.

Another key benefit of SBA 504 loans is the flexibility they offer in terms of eligible expenses. Small business owners can use these funds to purchase or construct new buildings, renovate existing facilities, or even refinance existing debt. This versatility allows healthcare professionals to tailor the loan to their specific needs, ensuring that they can grow and expand their practices in the most effective way possible.

Furthermore, SBA 504 loans come with longer repayment terms, often ranging from 10 to 25 years. This extended timeframe allows small business owners to manage their cash flow more effectively and reduces the strain on their day-to-day operations. With manageable monthly payments, healthcare professionals can focus on providing quality care to their patients without the added stress of high loan payments.

In summary, SBA 504 loans are a game-changer for small business owners in the healthcare industry. With low down payments, long-term fixed interest rates, flexibility in eligible expenses, and extended repayment terms, these loans provide the necessary financial support for primary care doctors, optometrists, dentists, and accountants to thrive and grow their practices. By leveraging the benefits of SBA 504 loans, healthcare professionals can invest in their future and create a solid foundation for long-term success.

Loan Amounts, Interest Rates, and Terms

Loan Amounts, Interest Rates, and Terms

When it comes to securing financing for your small healthcare business, understanding the loan amounts, interest rates, and terms is essential. The SBA 7a and 504 financing programs offer viable options for small business owners in the healthcare industry, including primary care doctors, optometrists, dentists, and accountants. Whether you're starting a new practice, expanding your existing one, or purchasing equipment, these programs provide accessible funding with favorable terms.

Loan amounts under the SBA 7a and 504 financing programs are attractive for small healthcare businesses. Depending on your specific needs, you can obtain loan amounts ranging from $50,000 to $5 million. This flexibility ensures that you can secure the necessary capital to meet your goals, whether it's upgrading your medical equipment or expanding your practice space. The loan amounts are determined based on your business's financials, collateral, and the purpose of the loan.

Interest rates are another crucial aspect of any loan. The SBA offers competitive interest rates for small healthcare businesses, often lower than traditional commercial loans. These rates are influenced by market conditions, the term of the loan, and your business's financial strength. By taking advantage of these lower rates, you can save on interest expenses and allocate those funds towards other aspects of your business, such as hiring qualified staff or investing in advanced technology.

The terms of SBA 7a and 504 financing are structured to suit the specific requirements of small healthcare businesses. The repayment terms can extend up to 25 years, depending on the purpose of the loan. This longer repayment period ensures that your monthly payments remain affordable, allowing you to allocate more funds towards growing your business. It's important to note that the terms may vary based on the specific lender and your financial profile, so it's advisable to consult with an experienced SBA loan specialist to determine the best terms for your unique situation.

In conclusion, SBA 7a and 504 financing programs offer attractive loan amounts, competitive interest rates, and favorable terms for small healthcare businesses. Whether you're a primary care doctor, optometrist, dentist, or accountant, these programs provide accessible funding options to meet your business goals. By understanding the loan amounts, interest rates, and terms, you can make informed decisions about financing your healthcare business and take the necessary steps towards success. Consult with an experienced SBA loan specialist who specializes in healthcare industry financing to navigate the process and secure the funding you need.

Eligible Expenses for SBA 504 Financing in Healthcare

Eligible Expenses for SBA 504 Financing in Healthcare

When it comes to financing your small business in the healthcare industry, understanding the eligible expenses for SBA 504 financing is crucial. The Small Business Administration (SBA) offers a range of loan programs designed to assist small business owners, including those in healthcare. By knowing which expenses are eligible for financing, you can make informed decisions and secure the funding you need to grow and thrive.

One of the main advantages of SBA 504 financing is its flexibility in covering various expenses. Whether you are a primary care doctor, optometrist, dentist, or accountant running a healthcare-related business, the eligible expenses for SBA 504 financing can help you achieve your goals. Here are some key expenses that can be covered:

1. Real estate acquisition: SBA 504 financing allows you to finance the purchase of commercial property for your healthcare practice. This includes office buildings, medical facilities, and even land for future expansion.

2. Construction or renovation: If you need to build or renovate your healthcare facility, SBA 504 financing can cover the costs associated with construction, remodeling, and improvements. This ensures that your space is tailored to your specific needs and meets the required healthcare standards.

3. Purchase of equipment: SBA 504 financing can be used to acquire essential medical equipment, such as diagnostic tools, imaging machines, dental chairs, and laboratory equipment. This allows you to provide top-notch care and stay competitive in the healthcare industry.

4. Working capital: In addition to tangible assets, SBA 504 financing can also be used for working capital needs. This includes covering payroll, inventory, marketing expenses, and other operational costs that are essential for the day-to-day running of your healthcare business.

5. Debt refinancing: If you have existing high-interest debt, SBA 504 financing can be used to refinance it at a lower interest rate. This helps to improve your cash flow and reduce financial stress, allowing you to focus on providing quality healthcare services.

It's important to note that there are certain limitations and requirements for each expense category. Consulting with an experienced lender or SBA expert is crucial to navigate the application process and ensure that you meet all the necessary criteria.

In conclusion, understanding the eligible expenses for SBA 504 financing in healthcare is vital for small business owners and healthcare professionals. By leveraging this financing option, you can obtain the necessary funds to acquire real estate, purchase equipment, renovate your facility, and cover working capital needs. Take advantage of the benefits SBA 504 financing offers and take your healthcare business to new heights.

Application Process for SBA 504 Loans in Healthcare

Application Process for SBA 504 Loans in Healthcare

When it comes to financing your small business in the healthcare industry, SBA 504 loans can be a game-changer. These loans, offered by the U.S. Small Business Administration (SBA), provide favorable terms and low interest rates, making them an attractive option for small business owners, including primary care doctors, optometrists, dentists, and accountants.

To successfully apply for an SBA 504 loan, there are a few steps that you need to follow. This subchapter will guide you through the application process, ensuring that you understand the requirements and can navigate the process with confidence.

The first step is to gather all the necessary documentation. This includes your personal financial statements, tax returns for the past three years, business financial statements, a detailed business plan, and any additional information that might be required by the lender. It's crucial to have these documents ready and organized to streamline the application process.

Next, you'll need to find a Certified Development Company (CDC) that specializes in SBA 504 loans for healthcare businesses. These CDCs work in partnership with traditional lenders and the SBA to provide financing to small businesses. Research and select a CDC that has experience in your niche of the healthcare industry, as they will have a better understanding of your unique needs.

Once you've chosen a CDC, you'll need to complete the loan application. This will involve providing detailed information about your business, including its history, structure, and financial projections. The CDC will review your application and determine if you meet the eligibility requirements for an SBA 504 loan.

If your application is approved, the CDC will work with you to prepare the necessary loan package. This includes completing the SBA forms, obtaining appraisals, and securing any additional collateral required. The CDC will guide you through this process, ensuring that all the paperwork is in order.

Finally, your loan package will be submitted to the SBA for final approval. The SBA will review the package and make a decision based on their criteria. If approved, the loan will be funded, and you can use the funds to grow your healthcare business.

Navigating the application process for SBA 504 loans in healthcare can be complex, but with the right guidance, it can be a smooth and successful journey. By understanding the requirements and working with experienced CDCs, small business owners in the healthcare industry can secure the financing they need to thrive and provide quality care to their patients.

Chapter 5: Choosing the Right Loan Program for Your Healthcare Business

Evaluating Your Healthcare Business's Financial Needs

Evaluating Your Healthcare Business's Financial Needs

One of the most important aspects of running a successful healthcare business is understanding and evaluating your financial needs. Whether you are a small business owner, primary care doctor, optometrist, dentist, or accountant, it is crucial to have a clear understanding of your financial requirements in order to ensure the growth and sustainability of your practice. This subchapter will dive into the key considerations and strategies for evaluating your healthcare business's financial needs, with a specific focus on SBA 7a and 504 financing for small businesses in the healthcare industry.

First and foremost, it is essential to conduct a comprehensive analysis of your current financial situation. This includes evaluating your revenue streams, expenses, and overall profitability. By understanding your financial position, you can identify any gaps or areas for improvement that may require additional funding.

Next, you should assess your business's growth potential and expansion plans. Are you looking to open a new practice, purchase new equipment, or hire additional staff? Identifying your growth objectives will help determine the amount of financing you may need and the type of loan that suits your needs.

Furthermore, understanding the specific requirements of SBA 7a and 504 financing is crucial. These loan programs are designed to support small businesses in the healthcare industry and provide favorable terms and conditions. By familiarizing yourself with the eligibility criteria, documentation requirements, and application process, you can better prepare to navigate the financing landscape.

Additionally, it is important to consider the long-term financial implications of any loan. Understanding the interest rates, repayment terms, and associated fees will allow you to evaluate the affordability and sustainability of the financing option. Working with a financial advisor or accountant who specializes in healthcare financing can provide valuable insights and guidance.

Finally, evaluating your healthcare business's financial needs should also involve assessing the potential risks and challenges that may impact your practice. By conducting a thorough risk assessment, you can proactively identify any threats to your financial stability and implement strategies to mitigate them.

In conclusion, evaluating your healthcare business's financial needs is a critical step towards achieving long-term success. By conducting a comprehensive analysis, understanding the requirements of SBA 7a and 504 financing, and considering the long-term implications, you can make informed decisions to support the growth and sustainability of your practice. Remember, seeking the guidance of professionals with expertise in healthcare financing can provide invaluable support throughout this process.

Assessing Your Business's Qualifications for SBA 7a vs. 504 Loans

Assessing Your Business's Qualifications for SBA 7a vs. 504 Loans

When it comes to financing options for small businesses in the healthcare industry, the Small Business Administration (SBA) offers two popular loan programs: SBA 7a and 504. These programs can provide the necessary capital to help your business grow and thrive. However, understanding the qualifications for each loan program is crucial in determining which one is the right fit for your specific business needs. In this subchapter, we will explore the key factors you need to consider when assessing your business's qualifications for SBA 7a vs. 504 loans.

SBA 7a loans are known for their flexibility and can be used for a variety of purposes, including working capital, refinancing existing debt, purchasing equipment, and even acquiring another business. These loans are typically easier to qualify for, making them a popular choice for small business owners in the healthcare industry. To assess whether your business qualifies for an SBA 7a loan, consider the following factors:

1. Creditworthiness: SBA 7a loans require a good credit score, usually above 680, to demonstrate your ability to repay the loan.

2. Collateral: While collateral may not be required for smaller loan amounts, larger loans may necessitate collateral in the form of business assets or personal guarantees.

3. Cash flow: Your business should have a positive cash flow that proves its ability to make regular loan payments.

On the other hand, SBA 504 loans are specifically designed to finance long-term fixed assets, such as real estate, land, and major equipment purchases. These loans offer low down payments and long repayment terms. To assess whether your business qualifies for an SBA 504 loan, consider the following factors:

1. Use of funds: SBA 504 loans can only be used for fixed assets or improvements that will benefit the business in the long term.

2. Job creation or economic development: This loan program prioritizes creating jobs or contributing to economic development within the community.

3. Financial stability: Your business should have a strong financial position and a positive outlook to demonstrate its ability to repay the loan.

By carefully evaluating your business's qualifications for SBA 7a vs. 504 loans, you can determine which program aligns best with your specific needs. It is always advisable to consult with an SBA-approved lender who specializes in healthcare financing to guide you through the application process and help you make an informed decision. Remember, choosing the right loan program can provide the necessary capital to fuel your business's growth and success in the healthcare industry.

Understanding the Impact of Loan Terms on Your Healthcare Business

Understanding the Impact of Loan Terms on Your Healthcare Business

When it comes to financing your healthcare business, understanding the impact of loan terms is crucial. Whether you are a small business owner, primary care doctor, optometrist, dentist, or accountant working in the healthcare industry, being well-informed about SBA 7a and 504 financing can make all the difference.

Loan terms play a significant role in determining the financial health and success of your healthcare business. They can impact your cash flow, profitability, and overall growth potential. Here are some key factors to consider:

1. Interest Rates: The interest rate on your loan will directly affect the cost of borrowing. Lower interest rates mean lower monthly payments and overall loan expenses. It is essential to shop around and compare rates from different lenders to secure the best possible deal for your healthcare business.

2. Loan Amount and Term: The loan amount and term determine the total repayment amount and the duration of the loan. Carefully assess your financial needs and repayment capacity to determine the right loan amount and term that aligns with your business goals. Longer terms may result in lower monthly payments but could also mean paying more interest over time.

3. Collateral and Personal Guarantees: Lenders often require collateral or personal guarantees to secure the loan. Collateral can include real estate, equipment, or other valuable assets. Personal guarantees hold individuals responsible for loan repayment in case the business is unable to meet its obligations. Understanding these requirements and their potential impact on your personal and business assets is essential.

4. Fees and Prepayment Penalties: Some loans may involve additional fees, such as origination fees or closing costs. Prepayment penalties can be a significant consideration, especially if you anticipate early repayment of the loan. Be sure to factor in these costs when evaluating loan options.

5. Flexibility and Terms: Different lenders offer different loan terms and conditions. Some lenders may offer more flexibility in terms of repayment schedules or refinancing options. Consider your future business plans and growth opportunities when choosing a loan that offers the necessary flexibility to meet your changing needs.

By understanding these loan terms and their impact, you can make informed decisions that align with your healthcare business's financial goals. Seeking the assistance of professionals specializing in SBA 7a and 504 financing for small businesses in the healthcare industry can provide invaluable guidance throughout the process.

Remember, securing the right loan terms can provide the financial foundation and flexibility needed to grow and thrive in the healthcare industry. Take the time to research, compare options, and consult with experts to ensure you make the best financing decisions for your healthcare business.

Comparing Interest Rates and Fees for SBA 7a and 504 Loans

Comparing Interest Rates and Fees for SBA 7a and 504 Loans

When it comes to securing financing for your small business in the healthcare industry, understanding the different loan options available is crucial. Two popular choices are the SBA 7a and 504 loans, both of which offer attractive interest rates and terms. In this subchapter, we will compare the interest rates and fees associated with these loans to help you make an informed decision.

The SBA 7a loan program is designed to provide funding for a wide range of small businesses, including those in the healthcare industry. These loans offer competitive interest rates, typically ranging from 5% to 8%. The exact rate you receive will depend on factors such as your credit score, business financials, and the current market conditions. Additionally, the SBA charges a guarantee fee, which is a one-time fee based on the loan amount. This fee can vary but generally falls between 2% to 3.75%.

On the other hand, the SBA 504 loan program is specifically tailored for the purchase of commercial real estate and major fixed assets. While these loans have slightly higher interest rates compared to the SBA 7a loans, they still offer favorable terms. The interest rates for SBA 504 loans are typically fixed and range from 4% to 6%. In addition to the interest rate, there are other fees associated with the SBA 504 loan program. These include a CDC processing fee, which is typically around 1.5% of the loan amount, and third-party closing costs.

When comparing the two loan programs, it's important to consider the purpose of your financing needs. If you require funds for working capital, inventory, or business expansion, the SBA 7a loan may be the better option due to its flexibility. However, if you are looking to purchase commercial real estate or invest in major fixed assets, the SBA 504 loan provides long-term, fixed-rate financing.

As a small business owner in the healthcare industry, it's crucial to weigh the interest rates and fees associated with SBA 7a and 504 loans. By understanding the differences between these loan programs, you can make an informed decision that aligns with your business goals and financial needs. Whether you're a primary care doctor, optometrist, dentist, or accountant, the SBA 7a and 504 financing options can provide the necessary funding to support your growth and success in the healthcare industry.

Chapter 6: Tips for a Successful Loan Application in Healthcare

Preparing Financial Documents and Projections

Preparing Financial Documents and Projections

In the world of small businesses in the healthcare industry, obtaining financing can be a crucial step towards growth and success. Whether you are a primary care doctor, optometrist, dentist, or accountant, understanding how to prepare financial documents and projections is essential when seeking SBA 7a and 504 financing. This subchapter will guide you through the process, providing valuable insights and tips to help you secure the funding you need.

Financial documents play a pivotal role in the loan application process. Lenders require these documents to assess your business's financial health and determine its ability to repay the loan. To begin, you must compile a comprehensive set of financial statements, including profit and loss statements, balance sheets, and cash flow statements. These statements should accurately reflect your business's financial standing, providing lenders with a clear picture of your revenue, expenses, assets, and liabilities.

In addition to financial statements, lenders often require projections for the future. Projections help lenders assess the viability of your business and its ability to generate sufficient cash flow to cover loan payments. When preparing projections, be realistic and conservative. Use historical data, market research, and industry trends to build a solid foundation for your estimates. Include income projections, expense projections, and cash flow projections for at least three years.

While preparing financial documents and projections may seem daunting, there are several strategies you can employ to streamline the process. First, consider engaging the services of a certified public accountant (CPA) or financial advisor with experience in the healthcare industry. Their expertise will ensure accuracy and enhance your credibility with lenders. Additionally, utilizing accounting software can simplify the process and help you generate professional financial statements and projections.

Remember that lenders are looking for evidence of your business's stability and potential for success. Take the time to thoroughly review and double-check all financial documents and projections before submitting them. Any errors or inconsistencies could raise red flags and jeopardize your chances of securing financing.

In conclusion, preparing financial documents and projections is a critical step when seeking SBA 7a and 504 financing in the healthcare industry. By compiling accurate and realistic financial statements and projections, you can demonstrate your business's financial health and potential for growth. Seek professional assistance, utilize accounting software, and double-check your documents to increase your chances of obtaining the funding you need to propel your business forward.

Building Solid Credit History and Score

Building Solid Credit History and Score

A strong credit history and score are crucial for small business owners in the healthcare industry who are seeking SBA 7a and 504 financing. Lenders use credit scores to assess the risk associated with lending money, and a solid credit history can significantly impact the success of loan applications. This subchapter will provide valuable insights and strategies to help small business owners in healthcare build and maintain a solid credit history and score.

1. Understanding Credit Scores: This section will explain the factors that influence credit scores, such as payment history, credit utilization, length of credit history, credit mix, and new credit. By understanding how credit scores are calculated, small business owners can make informed decisions to improve their scores.

2. Monitoring Credit Reports: Small business owners should regularly review their credit reports to identify any errors or discrepancies that may negatively impact their credit scores. This section will emphasize the importance of monitoring credit reports and provide tips on how to dispute inaccuracies.

3. Paying Bills on Time: Timely payment of bills is crucial for maintaining a positive credit history. This section will stress the significance of meeting payment deadlines and provide strategies for ensuring prompt payment, such as setting up automatic payments and reminders.

4. Managing Credit Utilization: Credit utilization refers to the percentage of available credit that is being utilized. Maintaining a low credit utilization ratio is essential for building a solid credit score. This section will discuss strategies for managing credit utilization, such as paying balances in full each month and avoiding maxing out credit cards.

5. Building a Lengthy Credit History: Lenders prefer borrowers with a lengthy credit history as it demonstrates their ability to manage credit responsibly. This section will provide tips for building a lengthy credit history, such as keeping old credit accounts open, avoiding unnecessary credit inquiries, and responsibly using credit over time.

6. Diversifying Credit Mix: A diverse credit mix, including credit cards, loans, and lines of credit, can positively impact credit scores. This section will explain the benefits of diversifying credit and provide guidance on how to responsibly manage various types of credit.

7. Seeking Professional Guidance: Small business owners in the healthcare industry can benefit from seeking professional guidance from accountants or credit counselors specializing in credit management. This section will highlight the value of professional advice and provide resources for finding reputable professionals.

By following the strategies outlined in this subchapter, small business owners in the healthcare industry can build a solid credit history and score, increasing their chances of securing SBA 7a and 504 financing for their businesses. A strong credit profile not only improves loan approval rates but also opens doors to better interest rates and more favorable loan terms.

Selecting the Right Lender for Your Healthcare Business

Selecting the Right Lender for Your Healthcare Business

When it comes to financing your healthcare business, choosing the right lender is crucial. The success and growth of your small business rely heavily on securing the right funding, and this is where SBA 7a and 504 financing come into play. As a small business owner in the healthcare industry, whether you are a primary care doctor, optometrist, dentist, or accountant, understanding the importance of selecting the right lender is essential.

SBA 7a and 504 financing are specifically designed to meet the unique needs of small businesses in the healthcare industry. These loan programs offer favorable terms, longer repayment periods, and lower interest rates compared to traditional loans. However, not all lenders are created equal, and finding the right one for your healthcare business is crucial. Here are some factors to consider when selecting the right lender:

1. Experience in healthcare financing: Look for lenders who specialize in providing financing solutions for healthcare businesses. Their expertise and understanding of the industry can make the loan process smoother and more efficient.

2. Reputation and track record: Research the lender's reputation and track record in the healthcare financing industry. Seek out reviews and testimonials from other healthcare professionals who have worked with them. A lender with a solid reputation is more likely to provide reliable and trustworthy service.

3. Flexibility and customized solutions: Each healthcare business has unique financing needs. Look for a lender who can offer flexible and customized solutions tailored to your specific requirements. This could include options for equipment financing, working capital, or practice acquisition.

4. Speed and efficiency: Time is of the essence when it comes to securing financing for your healthcare business. Choose a lender who can provide a quick turnaround time and efficient loan approval process. This will help you access the funds you need without unnecessary delays.

5. Support and guidance: Financing can be complex, especially for small business owners in the healthcare industry. Look for a lender who offers ongoing support and guidance throughout the loan process. A lender who understands the challenges and opportunities in the healthcare industry can provide valuable insights and advice.

By carefully considering these factors and selecting the right lender for your healthcare business, you can ensure that you have the necessary funding to support the growth and success of your small business. SBA 7a and 504 financing offer unique opportunities for small businesses in the healthcare industry, and finding the right lender can make all the difference in accessing these benefits. Take the time to research and choose a lender who understands your needs, provides customized solutions, and offers reliable support. With the right lender by your side, you can take your healthcare business to new heights.

Navigating the Application Process and Timelines

Navigating the Application Process and Timelines

When it comes to securing financing for your small business in the healthcare industry, understanding the application process and timelines is crucial. The SBA 7a and 504 financing options can be a game-changer for small business owners, primary care doctors, optometrists, dentists, and accountants looking to expand their healthcare practices. In this subchapter, we will guide you through the ins and outs of the application process, ensuring that you are well-prepared to take advantage of these financing opportunities.

The first step in navigating the application process is to gather all the necessary documentation. The SBA requires thorough financial statements, tax returns, business plans, and personal background information. Small business owners should be prepared to provide a detailed overview of their healthcare business, including its history, current operations, and future projections. This information will help the lender assess the viability of your business and determine the loan amount you qualify for.

Once you have gathered the required documents, it's time to approach a lender experienced in SBA 7a and 504 financing for the healthcare industry. These lenders understand the unique challenges and opportunities within the healthcare sector and can guide you through the application process. They will assist you in completing the necessary forms and ensure that all the information provided aligns with the lender's requirements.

Timing is crucial when it comes to applying for SBA loans. Familiarize yourself with the typical timelines involved in the application process, including the lender's review period, underwriting, and loan approval. It's important to start early and allow sufficient time for any potential delays. Remember, the SBA loan process can be complex, and being proactive will help you avoid unnecessary stress.

Additionally, understanding the various SBA loan programs available for healthcare businesses is essential. The SBA 7a program is designed to provide working capital, equipment financing, and real estate loans, while the 504 program focuses on long-term fixed asset financing, such as property and equipment purchases. By knowing which program suits your needs best, you can streamline the application process and increase your chances of approval.

In conclusion, navigating the application process and timelines for SBA 7a and 504 financing in the healthcare industry requires careful planning and organization. By gathering the necessary documentation, working with experienced lenders, adhering to timelines, and understanding the available loan programs, small business owners, primary care doctors, optometrists, dentists, and accountants can increase their chances of securing the financing needed to grow their healthcare practices. With the right guidance and preparation, you can take advantage of these financing opportunities and propel your healthcare business to new heights.

Chapter 7: Managing SBA 7a and 504 Loan Repayments in Healthcare

Understanding Loan Repayment Terms and Conditions

Understanding Loan Repayment Terms and Conditions

When it comes to securing financing for your small business in the healthcare industry, it is crucial to have a thorough understanding of the loan repayment terms and conditions. This subchapter aims to demystify the complexities surrounding loan repayment, providing small business owners, primary care doctors, optometrists, dentists, and accountants with the necessary knowledge to make informed decisions.

Loan repayment terms and conditions can vary depending on the type of financing you choose, such as SBA 7a or 504 loans. These loans are specifically designed to support small businesses in the healthcare industry, providing them with the necessary funds to expand their operations or invest in equipment and real estate.

One key aspect of loan repayment is the interest rate. This is the cost of borrowing the funds and is typically expressed as an annual percentage. SBA loans often offer competitive interest rates, making them an attractive option for small business owners in healthcare. However, it is important to carefully review the terms and conditions to ensure that the interest rate is favorable and manageable for your business.

Another crucial factor to consider is the loan term. This refers to the length of time you have to repay the loan. SBA loans usually offer longer repayment terms compared to traditional bank loans, allowing small business owners in healthcare to have more flexibility in managing their cash flow. However, it is essential to strike a balance between a longer repayment term and the total interest paid over the life of the loan.

Additionally, loan repayment terms and conditions may include prepayment penalties, which incur charges if the loan is paid off before the agreed-upon term. These penalties can vary, so it is important to carefully review the terms and conditions to avoid any unexpected costs.

Understanding loan repayment terms and conditions is vital for small business owners in the healthcare industry. By familiarizing yourself with these terms, you can make informed decisions about financing options that best suit your business needs. Whether you are a primary care doctor, optometrist, dentist, or accountant, having a comprehensive understanding of loan repayment terms and conditions will empower you to secure financing that supports the growth and success of your healthcare business.

Budgeting and Cash Flow Management for Healthcare Businesses

Budgeting and Cash Flow Management for Healthcare Businesses

Effective budgeting and cash flow management are crucial for the success and sustainability of small businesses in the healthcare industry. Whether you are a primary care doctor, optometrist, dentist, or accountant, understanding the intricacies of budgeting and cash flow management is essential to running a profitable healthcare business. This subchapter aims to provide valuable insights and strategies for small business owners in the healthcare sector, specifically focusing on SBA 7a and 504 financing.

Budgeting forms the foundation of financial planning for any healthcare business. It involves estimating and allocating resources, such as revenue, expenses, and investments, to achieve specific goals and objectives. Small business owners must create a comprehensive budget that includes all operational costs, such as rent, utilities, salaries, medical supplies, and marketing expenses. By accurately forecasting income and expenses, healthcare businesses can make informed decisions and ensure financial stability.

Cash flow management is equally important, as it involves monitoring the inflow and outflow of cash within a business. Small businesses in the healthcare industry often face unique challenges, such as delayed payments from insurance companies and managing accounts receivable. Efficient cash flow management involves streamlining billing and collection processes, negotiating favorable payment terms with suppliers, and implementing effective inventory management strategies. By optimizing cash flow, healthcare businesses can improve liquidity, cover operational expenses, and seize growth opportunities.

For small healthcare businesses seeking financing options, the SBA 7a and 504 loan programs can be highly beneficial. These programs provide attractive interest rates, longer repayment terms, and increased access to capital. However, obtaining SBA financing requires careful financial planning and meticulous documentation. This subchapter will guide small business owners through the process of applying for SBA loans, including the necessary paperwork, eligibility requirements, and strategies to increase the chances of approval.

In conclusion, budgeting and cash flow management are vital components of running a successful healthcare business. Small business owners, primary care doctors, optometrists, dentists, and accountants in the healthcare industry must prioritize financial planning to ensure profitability and growth. Moreover, understanding the intricacies of SBA 7a and 504 financing can provide small healthcare businesses with the necessary capital to expand their operations. By implementing effective budgeting and cash flow management strategies and leveraging SBA loan programs, small businesses in the healthcare sector can thrive in an ever-evolving industry.

Strategies for Loan Repayment and Debt Management

Strategies for Loan Repayment and Debt Management

Managing loan repayment and debt can be a challenging aspect of running a small business in the healthcare industry. However, with the right strategies in place, it is possible to navigate through these financial obligations effectively. This subchapter will provide small business owners, primary care doctors, optometrists, dentists, and accountants in the healthcare industry with insightful strategies for loan repayment and debt management under the SBA 7a and 504 financing programs.

1. Create a Budget: Developing a comprehensive budget is essential to understand your financial situation accurately. Assess your monthly cash flow, including income and expenses, to determine how much you can allocate towards loan repayment. By creating a realistic budget, you can plan your finances accordingly and ensure timely loan payments.

2. Prioritize Debt Repayment: Identify your debts and prioritize them based on interest rates and terms. Start by paying off high-interest loans first, as they accumulate more interest over time. Make consistent and timely payments to avoid penalties and ensure that you are reducing your overall debt burden.

3. Seek Loan Restructuring: If you find it challenging to meet your loan repayment obligations, consider seeking loan restructuring options. This may involve negotiating with your lender to extend the loan term or lower the interest rate. Restructuring can provide temporary relief and make your loan payments more manageable.

4. Explore Loan Forgiveness Programs: Research loan forgiveness programs available in the healthcare industry. Depending on your profession and location, there may be programs that offer partial or complete loan forgiveness in exchange for service in underserved areas or participation in specific initiatives. Taking advantage of these programs can significantly reduce your debt burden.

5. Refinance or Consolidate Debt: Evaluate the possibility of refinancing or consolidating your existing loans. This strategy can help you secure more favorable interest rates or combine multiple loans into a single manageable payment. Consider consulting with a financial advisor or loan specialist to explore this option further.

6. Increase Revenue and Reduce Expenses: Focus on increasing your revenue streams and reducing unnecessary expenses to free up more funds for loan repayment. Explore opportunities to expand your healthcare services, attract more patients, or negotiate better reimbursement rates with insurance providers. Additionally, analyze your expenses and identify areas where you can cut costs without compromising the quality of care.

By implementing these strategies for loan repayment and debt management, small business owners, primary care doctors, optometrists, dentists, and accountants in the healthcare industry can take control of their financial obligations. It is crucial to stay proactive, seek professional guidance when needed, and consistently monitor your progress towards becoming debt-free.

Dealing with Loan Default and Other Challenges

Dealing with Loan Default and Other Challenges

In the dynamic world of healthcare, small business owners, including primary care doctors, optometrists, dentists, and accountants, often face numerous challenges when it comes to securing financing for their businesses. Understanding and effectively dealing with loan default and other obstacles is crucial to the success and growth of their healthcare practices. This subchapter aims to provide valuable insights and strategies to navigate these challenges specifically within the context of SBA 7a and 504 financing for small businesses in the healthcare industry.

Loan default is a common concern for small business owners, and it's important to be proactive in addressing this issue. If you find yourself struggling to make loan payments, it's crucial to communicate with your lender as early as possible. Lenders are often willing to work with borrowers who are transparent and proactive in finding solutions. Exploring options such as loan modifications, deferments, or refinancing can help alleviate the burden of default and allow you to maintain a positive relationship with your lender.

Additionally, it's essential to have a thorough understanding of the terms and conditions of your loan agreement. Familiarize yourself with the specific default clauses, repayment schedules, and consequences of non-payment. By having a clear understanding of your obligations, you can plan and mitigate potential challenges in advance.

Another challenge that small business owners face is managing cash flow effectively. Healthcare businesses often experience fluctuations in revenue due to insurance reimbursements and patient volume. It's important to have a comprehensive financial management plan in place to ensure that you can meet your loan obligations during periods of lower cash flow. This may include building up an emergency fund, negotiating favorable payment terms with vendors, or implementing strategies to increase revenue during slower periods.

Furthermore, staying updated on industry trends, regulations, and best practices is crucial for healthcare professionals seeking SBA 7a and 504 financing. Understanding the unique requirements and opportunities within the healthcare industry can help you tailor your loan application and present a compelling case to lenders. Additionally, networking with other healthcare professionals and industry experts can provide valuable insights and potential partnership opportunities.

In conclusion, dealing with loan default and other challenges is an integral part of running a small business in the healthcare industry. By being proactive, communicating with your lender, and implementing sound financial management practices, you can navigate these challenges successfully. By staying informed and leveraging industry-specific knowledge, small business owners can increase their chances of securing SBA 7a and 504 financing, enabling them to grow and thrive in the ever-evolving healthcare landscape.

Chapter 8: Case Studies: Successful Healthcare Businesses with SBA Financing

Case Study 1: Dr. Smith's Primary Care Clinic

Case Study 1: Dr. Smith's Primary Care Clinic

In this chapter, we will delve into a fascinating case study that illustrates the power and potential of SBA 7a and 504 financing for small businesses in the healthcare industry. Our focus will be on Dr. Smith's Primary Care Clinic, a thriving medical practice that serves as a prime example of how this financing option can transform and enhance healthcare businesses.

Dr. Smith, a dedicated primary care physician, had a vision to establish a state-of-the-art clinic that would provide comprehensive healthcare services to the local community. However, like many small business owners in the healthcare industry, he faced significant financial challenges, particularly when it came to securing the necessary capital to realize his dream.

Fortunately, Dr. Smith discovered the SBA 7a and 504 financing programs, which are specifically designed to support small business owners in various sectors, including healthcare. These programs offer attractive loan terms, low interest rates, and flexible repayment options, making them a perfect fit for entrepreneurs like Dr. Smith.

With the help of an experienced SBA lender, Dr. Smith was able to secure the funding he needed to establish his primary care clinic. The SBA loan allowed him to cover the costs of purchasing or constructing the clinic building, acquiring essential medical equipment, and even hiring additional staff members.

Moreover, the SBA loan provided Dr. Smith with the financial stability to weather any unforeseen circumstances or challenges that may arise during the early stages of his clinic's operations. This security was especially crucial in the healthcare industry, where unexpected expenses and fluctuations in patient volume are not uncommon.

As a result of securing SBA financing, Dr. Smith's clinic flourished, attracting a growing number of patients and expanding its range of services. The additional revenue generated by the clinic allowed Dr. Smith to make regular loan repayments and gradually build equity in his business.

This case study serves as a testament to the transformative power of SBA 7a and 504 financing for small businesses in the healthcare industry. It highlights the potential for entrepreneurs to turn their dreams into reality, providing quality healthcare services to their communities while building a successful and sustainable business.

Whether you are a primary care doctor, optometrist, dentist, or accountant considering starting or expanding your healthcare business, the SBA 7a and 504 financing programs offer unique opportunities to access the capital you need. By exploring these options and working with experienced SBA lenders, you can pave the way for a prosperous future in the healthcare industry.

Case Study 2: OptiCare Vision Center

Case Study 2: OptiCare Vision Center

In this subchapter, we will delve into a fascinating case study that demonstrates the potential benefits of SBA 7a and 504 financing for small businesses in the healthcare industry. OptiCare Vision Center, a thriving optometry practice, serves as a prime example of how these financing programs can empower entrepreneurs and medical professionals alike.

OptiCare Vision Center, led by Dr. Sarah Thompson, had been operating successfully for over a decade, providing comprehensive eye care services to their community. However, Dr. Thompson faced a significant challenge when she decided to expand her practice to a larger facility to accommodate the growing demand for their services.

Understanding the financial constraints that come with expanding a business, Dr. Thompson decided to explore her options for financing. After extensive research and consultations with various financial experts, she discovered the immense potential of SBA 7a and 504 loans.

With the help of an experienced SBA lender, Dr. Thompson was able to secure an SBA 7a loan to finance the purchase of the new facility. This loan provided her with the necessary capital to acquire the property, renovate it to suit the needs of the practice, and purchase state-of-the-art equipment to enhance patient care.

Additionally, she utilized the SBA 504 loan program to finance a portion of the project cost. By combining the two loan programs, Dr. Thompson was able to access long-term, low-interest financing options that significantly reduced her upfront costs and monthly payments.

The benefits of SBA 7a and 504 financing did not stop there. Dr. Thompson found that the favorable loan terms allowed her to maintain a healthy cash flow while investing in the growth of her practice. The increased space and advanced equipment not only enhanced the patient experience but also attracted new clients and expanded the services offered.

This case study highlights how SBA 7a and 504 financing can be a game-changer for small businesses in the healthcare industry. Whether you are a primary care doctor, optometrist, dentist, or an accountant seeking to expand your practice, these financing programs can provide you with the capital you need to achieve your goals.

To learn more about how SBA 7a and 504 financing can benefit your healthcare business, make sure to read the subsequent chapters of this book. Explore the success stories of other healthcare entrepreneurs who have utilized these programs to unlock their growth potential. With the right financing, you too can take your business to new heights and provide exceptional care to your patients.

Case Study 3: Dental Solutions Group

Case Study 3: Dental Solutions Group

Introduction:

In this case study, we will explore the success story of Dental Solutions Group, a dental practice that leveraged SBA 7(a) and 504 financing to expand their business. This case study aims to provide small business owners in the healthcare industry, particularly primary care doctors, optometrists, dentists, and accountants, with insights into the benefits and opportunities offered by SBA 7(a) and 504 financing.

Background:

Dental Solutions Group, a reputable dental practice in the local community, had been serving patients for over a decade. However, they were facing challenges expanding their practice due to financial constraints. With a vision to offer a wider range of dental services and reach more patients, they sought out financing options that would support their growth objectives.

SBA 7(a) and 504 Financing:

Dental Solutions Group discovered the potential of SBA 7(a) and 504 financing, specifically tailored for small businesses in the healthcare industry. These financing options offered attractive terms, low down payments, and longer repayment periods, making them ideal for practices looking to expand or acquire new equipment.

The Application Process:

The practice reached out to a local SBA lender who specialized in healthcare financing. They guided Dental Solutions Group through the application process, assisting with the required documentation, financial statements, and business plans. The lender also helped them navigate the complexities of SBA regulations, ensuring a smooth and efficient application process.

Expansion and Growth:

With the approved SBA financing, Dental Solutions Group was able to expand their practice by acquiring a neighboring dental office and integrating new services, such as orthodontics and cosmetic dentistry. The funds also allowed them to invest in state-of-the-art equipment, technology, and training for their staff, enhancing their ability to serve patients effectively.

Results and Benefits:

Thanks to the SBA 7(a) and 504 financing, Dental Solutions Group experienced significant growth and increased revenue. The expanded services and improved facilities attracted a larger patient base, leading to higher patient satisfaction and repeat business. Additionally, the financing terms allowed the practice to manage cash flow effectively and repay the loan without straining their financial resources.

Conclusion:

The case study of Dental Solutions Group demonstrates the immense opportunities and benefits of SBA 7(a) and 504 financing for small businesses in the healthcare industry. By utilizing these financing options, small business owners in healthcare, such as primary care doctors, optometrists, dentists, and accountants, can achieve their growth aspirations, expand their practices, and provide better services to their patients. If you are a small business owner in the healthcare industry looking for financing solutions, consider exploring SBA 7(a) and 504 financing to realize your business's full potential.

Case Study 4: Accounting Solutions for Healthcare Providers

Case Study 4: Accounting Solutions for Healthcare Providers

In this subchapter, we will explore the accounting solutions available for healthcare providers, focusing on small businesses in the healthcare industry. Whether you are a primary care doctor, optometrist, dentist, or any other healthcare professional, understanding the financial aspects of your practice is crucial for its success. This case study aims to provide valuable insights into SBA 7a and 504 financing options specifically tailored for healthcare businesses.

One of the key challenges faced by healthcare providers is managing their finances effectively. With the ever-increasing complexities of healthcare regulations and reimbursements, it is vital to have a robust accounting system in place. This subchapter will delve into the various accounting solutions that can help streamline financial operations and optimize profitability.

Small business owners in the healthcare industry often struggle with cash flow management and maintaining accurate financial records. This case study will discuss how SBA 7a and 504 financing can provide the necessary funds to invest in accounting software and hire professional accountants. These solutions can help automate bookkeeping tasks, ensure compliance with tax regulations, and provide real-time insights into the financial health of your practice.

Additionally, we will explore the benefits of cloud-based accounting platforms that offer secure access to financial data from any device. Small business owners can benefit from these solutions by easily tracking expenses, invoicing patients, and generating financial reports. Moreover, we will discuss how these platforms integrate with electronic health records (EHR) systems, facilitating seamless data exchange between accounting and patient records.

This case study will also shed light on the importance of having a qualified accountant who specializes in the healthcare industry. Accountants with expertise in healthcare finance can assist in optimizing revenue cycles, analyzing financial statements, and developing strategies for growth. We will discuss how SBA 7a and 504 financing can help small businesses afford the services of experienced healthcare accountants.

To summarize, this subchapter will serve as a comprehensive guide for small business owners, primary care doctors, optometrists, dentists, and accountants in the healthcare industry. By understanding the accounting solutions available through SBA 7a and 504 financing, you can make informed decisions about managing your practice's finances. Implementing these solutions will not only streamline your accounting processes but also contribute to the overall success and sustainability of your healthcare business.

Chapter 9: Additional Resources and Support for Healthcare Businesses

Government Programs and Initiatives for Healthcare Businesses

Government Programs and Initiatives for Healthcare Businesses

As a small business owner in the healthcare industry, you may be aware of the challenges that come with financing your business. Whether you are a primary care doctor, optometrist, dentist, or accountant specializing in healthcare, understanding the various government programs and initiatives available to you can make a significant difference in obtaining the funding you need. In this subchapter, we will explore the benefits and opportunities provided by SBA 7a and 504 financing for small businesses in the healthcare industry.

The Small Business Administration (SBA) offers two primary financing programs that cater specifically to small businesses in the healthcare sector: the SBA 7a and 504 programs. These programs provide access to funding with attractive terms and conditions, ensuring that healthcare businesses can thrive and serve their communities effectively.

The SBA 7a program is a versatile financing option that can be used for various purposes, including working capital, equipment purchases, leasehold improvements, and even acquisition of existing healthcare practices. With a maximum loan amount of $5 million, competitive interest rates, and extended repayment terms, the SBA 7a program offers small business owners in healthcare the flexibility they need to grow and expand their operations.

On the other hand, the SBA 504 program focuses specifically on long-term fixed asset financing, such as real estate and major equipment purchases. This program provides small business owners with access to low down payments and long-term fixed-rate financing options, making it an ideal choice for healthcare businesses looking to invest in their own facilities or upgrade their equipment.

Both programs offer significant advantages over traditional financing options. They require less equity injection, making it easier for healthcare professionals to obtain the necessary funding. Additionally, the SBA guarantees a portion of the loan, reducing the risk for lenders and increasing their willingness to provide financing to healthcare businesses.

Understanding the intricacies of these programs is crucial for small business owners in the healthcare industry. By familiarizing yourself with the eligibility requirements, application process, and other essential details, you can position your business for success and secure the financing you need to thrive.

In the following chapters, we will delve deeper into the specifics of each program, providing valuable insights and guidance on how to navigate the application process successfully. With the right knowledge and access to government programs and initiatives, you can take your healthcare business to new heights and make a lasting impact on the community you serve.

Remember, as a small business owner in the healthcare industry, you don't have to face financing challenges alone. The SBA 7a and 504 programs are here to support you, offering opportunities for growth, expansion, and enhanced patient care.

Partnering with Industry Associations and Organizations

Partnering with Industry Associations and Organizations

In the fast-paced and ever-evolving healthcare industry, small business owners, primary care doctors, optometrists, dentists, and accountants face numerous challenges when it comes to securing financing for their ventures. The good news is that there are several resources available to help navigate the complex world of SBA 7a and 504 financing in healthcare.

One valuable avenue to explore is partnering with industry associations and organizations. These entities play a crucial role in supporting and advocating for businesses in the healthcare sector, providing a wealth of knowledge, networking opportunities, and access to financing options specifically tailored to the industry's unique needs.

By actively engaging with industry associations, small business owners and healthcare professionals can tap into a wealth of resources and benefits. These associations often have established relationships with lenders and financial institutions that specialize in SBA 7a and 504 financing for small businesses in the healthcare industry. They can help connect borrowers with these lenders, streamlining the loan application process and increasing the chances of approval.

Moreover, industry associations offer a platform for knowledge sharing and professional development. Through conferences, seminars, and workshops, small business owners and healthcare professionals can stay up-to-date with the latest industry trends, best practices, and regulatory changes. This knowledge can be invaluable when preparing loan applications and presenting a compelling case to lenders.

Another advantage of partnering with industry associations is the opportunity to build a strong professional network. By connecting with fellow healthcare professionals, small business owners can gain insights from experienced industry veterans, collaborate on joint ventures, and even find potential business partners. These connections can open doors to new financing opportunities and help entrepreneurs overcome common challenges in the healthcare sector.

Additionally, industry associations often have advocacy programs in place to support their members. They work closely with government agencies, policymakers, and regulatory bodies to address industry-specific issues and promote favorable policies that benefit small businesses in healthcare. By aligning with these associations, small business owners and healthcare professionals can amplify their voices and influence positive change in the financing landscape.

In conclusion, partnering with industry associations and organizations is a smart move for small business owners, primary care doctors, optometrists, dentists, and accountants seeking SBA 7a and 504 financing in the healthcare industry. By leveraging the resources, knowledge, and network provided by these associations, entrepreneurs can increase their chances of securing the funding they need to grow and thrive in the dynamic healthcare sector.

Professional Services and Consultants for Healthcare Businesses

Professional Services and Consultants for Healthcare Businesses

Running a successful healthcare business requires more than just medical expertise. It requires a deep understanding of the financial and operational aspects of the industry. That's where professional services and consultants come into play. In this subchapter, we will explore the importance of professional services and consultants for healthcare businesses and how they can help small business owners, primary care doctors, optometrists, dentists, and accountants navigate the complex world of SBA 7a and 504 financing.

One of the key benefits of engaging professional services and consultants is their expertise in the healthcare industry. They have a deep understanding of the financial challenges and opportunities specific to healthcare businesses. Whether you are a small business owner looking to expand your practice or a primary care doctor aiming to start your own clinic, these professionals can provide tailored advice and guidance to help you achieve your goals.

Professional services and consultants can assist in various areas, including financial planning, accounting, tax compliance, and business valuation. They can analyze your financial statements, identify areas for improvement, and help you develop a comprehensive financial plan that aligns with your business objectives. Additionally, they can guide you through the intricacies of SBA 7a and 504 financing, ensuring that you make informed decisions and maximize the benefits available to you.

For optometrists and dentists, professional services and consultants can offer specialized assistance. They can help you understand the specific challenges and opportunities in your field, such as equipment financing or practice acquisition. With their industry-specific knowledge, they can provide valuable insights and help you navigate the intricacies of SBA 7a and 504 financing for healthcare businesses.

Accountants also play a crucial role in the success of healthcare businesses. They can assist with financial record-keeping, tax planning, and compliance, ensuring that your business remains in good standing with the IRS. Moreover, accountants can help you optimize your financial structure and identify opportunities for cost savings and increased profitability.

In conclusion, professional services and consultants are invaluable resources for small business owners, primary care doctors, optometrists, dentists, and accountants in the healthcare industry. They bring industry-specific expertise and can guide you through the complexities of SBA 7a and 504 financing. By leveraging their knowledge and experience, you can make well-informed decisions that will drive the growth and success of your healthcare business.

Continuing Education and Training Opportunities in Healthcare Financing

Continuing Education and Training Opportunities in Healthcare Financing

As the healthcare industry continues to evolve, it is crucial for small business owners and healthcare professionals to stay updated with the latest trends and knowledge in healthcare financing. Understanding the ins and outs of SBA 7a and 504 financing can greatly benefit those in the healthcare industry, such as primary care doctors, optometrists, dentists, and accountants.

Continuing education and training opportunities provide invaluable resources for small business owners and healthcare professionals to enhance their understanding of healthcare financing. By staying informed, they can make more informed decisions and navigate the complexities of SBA 7a and 504 financing with confidence.

One excellent resource for continuing education in healthcare financing is attending industry-specific conferences and seminars. These events bring together experts in the field, providing insights into the latest regulations, funding options, and success stories. Small business owners and healthcare professionals can network with peers, exchange ideas, and learn from one another's experiences.

Furthermore, there are numerous online courses and webinars tailored to healthcare financing. These resources offer the flexibility to learn at your own pace and convenience. Topics covered may include loan structuring, financial analysis, loan eligibility criteria, and the application process for SBA 7a and 504 financing. By taking advantage of these online courses, small business owners and healthcare professionals can gain a comprehensive understanding of healthcare financing without disrupting their busy schedules.

Additionally, professional associations and organizations within the healthcare industry often provide valuable educational resources. These associations offer workshops, publications, and webinars that focus specifically on healthcare financing. By becoming a member, small business owners and healthcare professionals gain access to a wealth of information, as well as networking opportunities with industry experts and peers.

Lastly, consulting with financial advisors who specialize in healthcare financing can provide personalized guidance and insights. These advisors can help small business owners and healthcare professionals navigate the loan application process, identify the best financing options, and optimize their financial strategies for growth.

In conclusion, continuing education and training opportunities play a crucial role in ensuring small business owners, primary care doctors, optometrists, dentists, and accountants in the healthcare industry are well-equipped to navigate the complexities of healthcare financing. By staying informed and up to date on the latest trends and regulations, they can make informed decisions that will benefit their businesses and patients alike. Whether through attending conferences and seminars, online courses, professional associations, or seeking guidance from financial advisors, ongoing education is essential for success in the ever-evolving landscape of SBA 7a and 504 financing in the healthcare industry.

Chapter 10: Conclusion

Recap of Key Points and Takeaways

Recap of Key Points and Takeaways

As small business owners in the healthcare industry, understanding the intricacies of SBA 7a and 504 financing is crucial for your success. In this subchapter, we will recap the key points and takeaways discussed throughout "The Ultimate Guide to SBA 7a and 504 Financing in Healthcare."

First and foremost, it is essential to grasp the basics of SBA 7a and 504 loans. The SBA 7a loan program provides small businesses with flexible funding options, including working capital, equipment purchases, and real estate investments. On the other hand, the SBA 504 loan program focuses mainly on real estate and long-term fixed asset financing.

One of the most critical takeaways for small business owners in healthcare is the unique eligibility criteria for SBA loans. Understanding the specific requirements and qualifications can significantly increase your chances of securing the financing you need. Factors such as credit score, business experience, and financial documentation play a vital role in the approval process.

Moreover, it is crucial to comprehend the advantages and benefits of SBA loans for healthcare businesses. These loans typically offer longer repayment terms, lower down payments, and competitive interest rates. By utilizing SBA 7a and 504 financing, you can acquire the necessary funds to expand your practice, purchase medical equipment, or even construct a new facility.

For primary care doctors, optometrists, and dentists, the SBA 7a and 504 loan programs present unique opportunities. Take note of the specific guidelines for healthcare professionals, including the maximum loan amounts and the importance of a solid business plan. Tailoring your loan application to meet these requirements can significantly increase your chances of approval.

Lastly, it is crucial for accountants and financial advisors to understand the ins and outs of SBA 7a and 504 financing in the healthcare industry. By guiding your clients through the loan application process, you can help them secure the necessary funds to grow their practices and achieve their financial goals.

In summary, "The Ultimate Guide to SBA 7a and 504 Financing in Healthcare" emphasizes the importance of understanding the key points and takeaways regarding SBA loans. By familiarizing yourself with the eligibility criteria, advantages, and tailored guidelines for healthcare professionals, you can make informed decisions and increase your chances of successful financing. Whether you are a small business owner, primary care doctor, optometrist, dentist, or accountant, this comprehensive guide equips you with the knowledge necessary to navigate the world of SBA 7a and 504 financing in the healthcare industry.

Final Thoughts on SBA 7a and 504 Financing in Healthcare

Final Thoughts on SBA 7a and 504 Financing in Healthcare

As we come to the end of this comprehensive guide on SBA 7a and 504 financing in the healthcare industry, it is important to reflect on the key takeaways and insights that can benefit small business owners, primary care doctors, optometrists, dentists, and accountants in this niche.

The healthcare industry is unique, with its own set of challenges and opportunities. SBA 7a and 504 financing offer small businesses in healthcare a chance to secure funding and grow their practices, expand their facilities, or invest in new equipment. These financing programs provide favorable terms and conditions that can significantly benefit healthcare professionals and small business owners.

Throughout this guide, we have explored the various aspects of SBA 7a and 504 financing, including eligibility criteria, loan terms, application process, and the benefits they offer. We have highlighted the specific requirements and considerations for healthcare businesses, ensuring you have the necessary knowledge to navigate this complex landscape.

One crucial aspect we discussed is the importance of a well-prepared loan application. Small business owners and healthcare professionals must present a compelling case to lenders, showcasing their industry expertise, business plans, and financial projections. By understanding the specific requirements of SBA 7a and 504 financing, you have the opportunity to present a strong application that increases your chances of approval.

Moreover, we emphasized the significance of building strong relationships with both lenders and industry professionals. Networking and seeking guidance from accountants, who understand the healthcare industry's financial intricacies, can prove invaluable in securing the right financing for your business. Additionally, connecting with fellow healthcare professionals can provide insights, advice, and potential partnerships that can further enhance your growth prospects.

Lastly, we encourage you to stay informed about the ever-changing landscape of SBA 7a and 504 financing. Regulations and guidelines may evolve, and being up-to-date with the latest developments will allow you to take advantage of new opportunities and adapt your business strategy accordingly.

In conclusion, SBA 7a and 504 financing present a powerful tool for small businesses in the healthcare industry to achieve their growth objectives. By leveraging the knowledge and insights shared in this guide, small business owners, primary care doctors, optometrists, dentists, and accountants can navigate the world of healthcare financing with confidence and secure the funding needed to thrive in this dynamic industry.

Empowering Small Business Owners in the Healthcare Industry

Empowering Small Business Owners in the Healthcare Industry

The healthcare industry is a vital sector of the economy, and small businesses within this industry play a crucial role in providing essential services to communities. However, small business owners in the healthcare industry often face numerous challenges when it comes to financing their operations and expanding their practices. This subchapter aims to address these challenges and provide valuable insights on how small business owners in healthcare can empower themselves through SBA 7a and 504 financing.

SBA 7a and 504 financing are government-backed loan programs specifically designed to support small businesses in various industries, including healthcare. These programs offer numerous advantages, such as lower down payments, longer repayment terms, and competitive interest rates. By utilizing these financing options, small business owners in the healthcare industry can overcome barriers to growth and achieve their business goals.

One of the major benefits of SBA 7a and 504 financing is the accessibility it provides to small business owners. Traditional lenders often hesitate to provide loans to healthcare businesses due to perceived risks. However, with SBA backing, lenders are more willing to extend credit to small business owners in this industry. This opens up opportunities for primary care doctors, optometrists, dentists, and other healthcare professionals to secure the funding necessary to expand their practices, invest in new equipment, or hire additional staff.

Moreover, SBA loans offer flexible terms and can be tailored to meet the unique needs of healthcare businesses. Whether a small business owner wants to purchase a new office space, renovate an existing facility, or acquire advanced medical equipment, SBA financing can accommodate these requirements. The longer repayment terms and lower down payments help small business owners manage their cash flow effectively and ensure that their business operations continue smoothly.

Additionally, this subchapter will provide insights on how accountants specializing in healthcare can assist small business owners in navigating the SBA loan process. Accountants play a vital role in helping healthcare businesses maintain accurate financial records, which is crucial when applying for SBA financing. They can also provide guidance on financial planning and tax strategies to maximize the benefits of SBA loans.

In conclusion, SBA 7a and 504 financing offer a wealth of opportunities for small business owners in the healthcare industry. This subchapter aims to empower small business owners, primary care doctors, optometrists, dentists, and accountants by providing valuable information on how to leverage SBA loans to grow their businesses, overcome financial challenges, and contribute to the overall well-being of their communities. With the right financing and guidance, small business owners in healthcare can thrive and continue providing essential services to those in need.

About the Author

Carl Cuesta is a full time father and commercial realtor. His hobbies include spending time with family and practicing Brazilian Jiu Jitsu. He loves God, his country and his fellow man and aims to elevate the lives of everyone around him.

Learn more at:

www.HoustonRealtorDad.com

www.ingramcontent.com/pod-product-compliance
Lightning Source LLC
Chambersburg PA
CBHW062354290526
45794CB00005B/2225